Wheelchair Road Racing

by James R. Little, Ph.D.

Content Consultant:

Barry M. Ewing

Chairman

Wheelchair Sports, USA

RiverFront Books

An Imprint of Franklin Watts
A Division of Grolier Publishing
New York   London   Hong Kong   Sydney
Danbury, Connecticut

Library of Congress Cataloging-in-Publication Data
Little, James R.
    Wheelchair road racing / by James R. Little
        p.   cm. -- (Wheelchair sports)
    Includes bibliographical references (p. 44) and index.
    Summary: Describes the history of the sport of wheelchair road
racing, as well as the training, equipment, and rules involved.
    ISBN 1-56065-615-8
    1. Wheelchair road racing--Juvenile literature. [1. Wheelchair
road racing. 2. Sports for the physically handicapped.] I. Title.
II. Series.
GV1084.L58 1998
796.6'087'3--dc21   97-15071
                                                  CIP
                                                  AC

Editorial Credits

Editor, Greg Linder; cover design and logo, Timothy Halldin; photo
    research, Michelle L. Norstad

Photo Credits

Sports 'N Spokes/Paralyzed Veterans of America, cover, 8-9, 15, 17,
    32, 36, 40-41; Jeffrey Milne, 4; Curt Beamer, 23, 26, 34; Delfina
    Colby, 30

Betty Crowell, 6

Unicorn Stock/Tommy Dodson, 10; Robin Rudd, 18; W. Keith
    McMakin, 12; Aneal S. Vohra,39, 47

Harry M. Walker, 20, 28

Tom Pantages, 24

Bob Firth, 39

Special thanks to *Sports 'N Spokes*/Paralyzed Veterans of America and
Wheelchair Sports, USA, for their assistance.

Table of Contents

Chapter 1
Off to the Races

An official fires the starting gun. As many as 50 wheelchair racers push off from the starting line. The road race has started with a bang.

There are two kinds of wheelchair races. Wheelchair track races are held on tracks built just for racing. Wheelchair road races happen on streets and highways. Both kinds of races can include runners, wheelchair racers, or both.

Road racing is a popular sport. More than 200 official wheelchair road races are held in the United States each year. Official races are

Wheelchair road races happen on streets and highways.

Top wheelchair racers are faster than runners in distances of mo **than one mile (1.6 kilometers).**

races approved by an organization called
Wheelchair Sports, USA.

Road races cover many distances. Some are
as short as one mile (1.6 kilometers). The
longest road race is the marathon. A marathon
covers 26 miles, 385 yards (about 42
kilometers). The distance of other races is
measured in kilometers instead of miles. These

races cover five kilometers (about three miles), 10 kilometers (about six miles), or 15 kilometers (about nine miles).

Many runners and wheelchair racers belong to clubs. Over 600 clubs are part of The Road Runners Clubs of America. Each club holds its own races. During warm weather, a club may hold a race every week.

Top wheelchair racers are faster than runners in distances of over one mile. Most road races are at least three miles long. So the first-place wheelchair racer usually finishes the race ahead of every runner.

The best wheelchair athletes can win thousands of dollars in prize money. An athlete is a person trained in a sport or a game.

The best wheelchair road racers can win thousands of dollars in prize money.

Chapter 2
History

Wheelchair road racing started in the early 1970s. It is a new sport compared to other wheelchair sports. Wheelchair archery, basketball, and bowling have been popular for about 50 years. Wheelchair swimming, tennis, and weight lifting have been around for about that long, too.

The First Racers
At one time, many people believed that wheelchair users were weak. Even doctors thought that wheelchair users should not perform

sports. The first wheelchair road racers had to prove they were strong enough to compete.

The first racers competed in short races that were only for runners. The wheelchair athletes could not officially enter these races. But they soon proved they could finish the races quickly and safely.

By the mid-1970s, race directors had set up a wheelchair division at many road races. At that time, wheelchair athletes were not allowed to enter road races longer than one mile (1.6 kilometers). But male and female wheelchair racers soon attempted ten-kilometer races. Again, they proved to race directors and athletes that they could go the distance.

Marathon Races

Marathons are the longest road races. These races started more than 2,000 years ago.

In 490 B.C., Greek soldiers won a battle at the Greek town of Marathon. A soldier named Pheidippides (fy-DIP-uh-deez) reported the

Wheelchair athletes proved they were strong enough to compete in races.

victory by running to the capital city of Athens. He delivered his good news to the Greek king. Then the worn out runner fell over and died. Afterward, the distance between the two cities was used as the length for foot races. The races were called marathons.

Modern marathons are held in cities throughout the world. Each race brings athletes and thousands of visitors to the city where the event occurs.

Until the mid-1970s, people who set up modern marathons did not want wheelchair athletes to compete. They thought wheelchair racers would get hurt. They feared that marathon runners would be hurt by the wheelchairs. Again, wheelchair racers had to prove that they could compete safely.

Bob Hall of Boston was the first wheelchair racer to enter the famous Boston Marathon. He raced in 1975, using a heavy 50-pound (22 and one half-kilogram) wheelchair. Hall completed the race in two hours, 58 minutes.

Wheelchair racers had to prove that they could compete safely in marathons.

The winning times for racers have improved as wheelchairs have become lighter. The best time for a wheelchair racer in the 1997 Boston Marathon was just one hour, 28 minutes, and 14 seconds.

Many of the best wheelchair racers compete in the marathon held during the Paralympic Games. Like the Olympic Games, the Paralympics are sports contests for athletes from many countries. But the athletes at the Paralympics are people with disabilities. A person with disabilities is a person who has a permanent illness, injury, or birth defect. A permanent disability is a disability that cannot be fixed or cured.

Bob Hall made history back in 1975. Since then, wheelchair racers have gained the respect of the sports world.

Bob Hall made history when he entered the famous Boston Marathon.

Chapter 3

The Road Race

The route chosen for a race is called the race course. For safety reasons, a race course should not have curbs, potholes, or large bumps. However, the race course may include steep hills and sweeping curves.

Roads with smooth surfaces work best for road races. The roads are marked with cones or safety signs. During most races, cars and trucks are not allowed to travel on the race course.

Racers must stay on the course at all times. They must use wheelchairs and equipment

Racers must use approved wheelchairs and equipment.

approved by the organization that governs the race. Racers who do not obey the rules are disqualified. Disqualified means not allowed to compete.

Wheelchair racers start 10 to 30 minutes before runners. This helps prevent accidents at the crowded starting line.

Passing

Wheelchair racers must pass each other safely. A racer who is passing must not slow down, block, or bump into other racers.

An athlete passing another racer must be ahead of that racer by a full wheel width. Only then can the passing racer pull in front of the other racer.

Drafting

Air slows down any moving object, including a wheelchair racer. The force of the air that slows down a moving object is called air resistance. The faster the object is moving, the greater the air resistance.

Drafting helps racers reduce air resistance.

To reduce air resistance, wheelchair racers draft. Drafting means following closely behind another racer.

The racer in front pushes the wheelchair at high speed. This racer works hard to overcome air resistance. A pocket of air behind the racer offers much less resistance. A second racer drafts by staying in that pocket of air. The second racer uses less effort because there is less air resistance. During a race, smart racers save energy by drafting.

Race Sponsors

Road races may be planned by businesses, city and state governments, or road racing clubs. Many races have sponsors. A sponsor is a business that helps pay the expenses of a race or an athlete.

Some sponsors pay to bring well-known wheelchair racers to their races. Companies that build racing chairs often sponsor top racers. The racers use chairs made by the sponsoring company. The company hopes other athletes will want to buy the same chairs.

Sponsors sometimes pay to bring well-known athletes to road races.

Chapter 4

Wheelchair Racers

Every year, more wheelchair athletes become road racers. The sport is fun and challenging. Road racing is also a great way to strengthen the upper body.

Many wheelchair racers are paraplegics. Paraplegics are people who have little or no ability to move the lower part of their bodies. Some racers have lost one or both legs due to amputation. Amputation means the removal of an arm or leg.

Some racers have lost one or both legs due to amputation.

Who Can Race?

A wheelchair road racer must have a permanent disability in one or both legs. People with temporary disabilities are not allowed to compete.

Wheelchair racers are divided into four classes. Those in class T1 are the most severely disabled. They are quadriplegics. A quadriplegic is a person who has limited ability to move the upper and lower parts of the body.

Athletes in class T4 are the least disabled. Most are paraplegics who have some control over their leg and foot muscles. Their arms and upper bodies are usually quite strong.

At a road race, athletes compete against others in their class. Men compete against men, and women compete against women. The idea is to make every race as fair as possible.

Wheelchair Sports, USA, suggests that all racers should be at least 12 years old. But racers as young as eight years old sometimes

At a race, athletes compete against others in their class.

compete. These young athletes compete in races that cover no more than 10 kilometers.

Training

Wheelchair racers must have a safe place to train. Because of traffic, many public roads are not safe. Traffic is the movement of cars, trucks, and buses on roads. To be safer, some athletes train on bicycle trails.

Racers train like long distance runners. They practice by racing for long distances. Some wheelchair racers cover 100 miles (160 kilometers) or more per week. Most racers practice racing every other day. On the days in between, they do muscle stretches and other light exercises.

Wheelchair racers try to strengthen their arm and shoulder muscles, their hearts, and their lungs. Many athletes lift weights. They plan training programs with their coaches. Following a training program is hard work. But

Most public roads are not safe places for wheelchair athletes to train.

those who train improve their speed and their racing times.

Wheelchair athletes try to be in peak condition at the time of important races. Most top racers limit themselves to one marathon race per month. This gives their muscles time to recover after each race.

Jean Driscoll won the Boston Marathon women's wheelchair race seven times in a row. She has trained with the best male racers. She improved her speed by working to keep up with these racers. Driscoll has finished marathons in about one hour, 32 minutes.

Jean Driscoll won the Boston Marathon women's wheelchair race seven times in a row.

Chapter 5

Equipment and Safety

Auto racers want to drive the fastest cars. Wheelchair racers want to use the fastest wheelchairs.

Racing chairs have become lighter and faster. In the 1970s, racing chairs often weighed 50 pounds (about 22 kilograms). Today's racing chairs weigh as little as 12 pounds (about five and one-half kilograms). They are made of metals that are strong but lightweight.

Because racing chairs are customized, they are expensive. A customized chair is a wheelchair that is exactly the right size and

Today's racing chairs are lighter and faster than ever before.

shape for its user. A wheelchair racer might pay $2,000 for a customized racing chair.

Using a chair that doesn't fit could slow a wheelchair racer down. It could even result in getting hurt during a race.

Parts of a Racing Chair

Racing chairs are built to travel quickly and safely. A racing chair has two bicycle-sized rear wheels. The wheels are 28 inches (70 centimeters) across. They are inflated to make them travel faster. Inflated means filled with air.

Older racing chairs had two small front wheels. Later, wheelchair builders made the front wheels larger. Today, racing chairs have just one wheel in front. Racing chairs have gone from four wheels to three.

Racers move their chairs by pushing on the pushrims. A pushrim is a metal tube or rim attached to the outside of each rear wheel. The

Racing chairs have gone from four wheels to three.

pushrim is smaller than the wheel. Each rim is about one-half inch (1.27 centimeters) wide.

Top athletes reach speeds of about 50 miles (80 kilometers) per hour when they are traveling downhill. The racers are often bunched together. For safety reasons, a bicycle brake is attached to each racing chair. The brake can stop or slow down the chair's front wheel. Racers avoid many crashes by using the brake.

Racers steer their chairs by turning the front wheel. They turn the wheel with a steering handle. This is a metal bar or lever attached near the front wheel.

Steering systems are sometimes called compensators. These systems help racers keep their wheelchairs going in a straight line. Compensators use small, easy to reach handles. Racers can move the handles with quick hand movements.

Top racers reach speeds of about 50 miles (80 kilometers) per hour.

Racing chairs are built as narrow as possible. This is done to reduce air resistance. For safety, chairs have side guards and fenders. These metal shields keep racers' bodies and clothing away from the moving wheels.

Racers often attach a small computer to their racing chair. The computer shows how fast a wheelchair racer is going. It displays how much time has passed since the race started. It tells how much distance a racer has covered. Some computers even measure how fast a racer's heart is beating. The computer helps a racer keep a safe, steady pace throughout the race.

Racing Equipment

Road racers are required to wear gloves. The gloves protect their hands from sores and bruises. Racers must also use safety helmets to protect their heads.

Racers wear tight-fitting uniforms like those worn by bicycle racers. The uniforms are made of very thin fabric. This helps racers fit easily into their chairs. The thin fabric helps reduce air resistance, too.

The best wheelchair racers are both fast and careful.

Racing chairs are strong, but they can break down. Because of this, racers must have a repair kit and tools.

Safety and speed are the most important elements of wheelchair road racing. The best wheelchair racers are both fast and careful.

uniform

rear wheels

gloves

helmet

pushrim

side guard

front
wheel

Words to Know

air resistance (AIR ri-ZISS-tuhnss)—the force of the air that slows down a moving object

amputation (am-pyoo-TAY-shun)—the removal of an arm or leg

athlete (ATH-leet)—a person trained in a sport or a game

compensator (KOM-puhn-say-tur)—a steering system on a racing chair

customized wheelchair (KUHSS-tum-ized WEEL-chair)—a wheelchair that is exactly the right size and shape for its user

disqualified (diss-KWOL-uh-fyed)—not allowed to compete

drafting (DRAF-ting)—following close behind another racer

marathon (MAR-uh-thon)—a race that covers about 42 kilometers (26 miles, 385 yards)

Paralympic Games (pa-ruh-LIM-pik GAMES)—sports contests for athletes from many countries; the athletes are people with disabilities

paraplegic (pa-ruh-PLEE-jik)—a person who has little or no ability to move the lower part of the body

permanent disability (PUR-muh-nuhnt diss-uh-BIL-uh-tee)—a disability that cannot be fixed or cured

person with disabilities (PUR-suhn WITH diss-uh-BIL-uh-teez)—someone who has a permanent illness, injury, or birth defect

pushrim (PUSH-rim)—a metal tube or rim attached to the outside of a racing chair's rear wheel

quadriplegic (kwahd-ruh-PLEE-jik)—a person who has limited ability to move the upper and lower parts of the body

race course (RAYSS KORSS)—the route chosen for a race

sponsor (SPON-sur)—a business that helps pay the expenses of a race or an athlete

steering handle (STIHR-ing HAN-duhl)—a metal bar or lever used to steer a racing chair

traffic (TRAF-ik)—the movement of cars, trucks, and buses on roads

To Learn More

Savitz, Harriet May. *Wheelchair Champions.*
New York: Crowell, 1978.

Weisman, Marilee and Jan Godfrey. *So Get on
with It: A Celebration of Wheelchair Sports.*
Toronto: Doubleday Canada, 1976.

You can learn more about wheelchair road racing
in *Sports 'N Spokes* magazine.

Useful Addresses

Wheelchair Sports, USA
3595 East Fountain Boulevard
Colorado Springs, CO 80910

Canadian Wheelchair Sports Association
1600 James Naismith Drive
Gloucester, ON K1B 5N4
Canada

Mexican Wheelchair Sport Program
Federacion Mexicana de Deportes Sobre
Silla de Ruedas y Rehabilitados AC
Edificio Codeme Cubiculo 306
Puerta 9 CD Deportiva
Mexico 08010 DF

Internet Sites

Canadian Wheelchair Sports Association
http://indie.ca:80/cwsa/index.html

University of Illinois Wheelchair Sports
http://www.als.uiuc.edu/dres/wc-sports

Wheelchair Racing Resource Page
http://www.execpc.com/~birzer

The Jean Driscoll Story
http://www.fea.org/stv-apr97/driscoll.html

Index